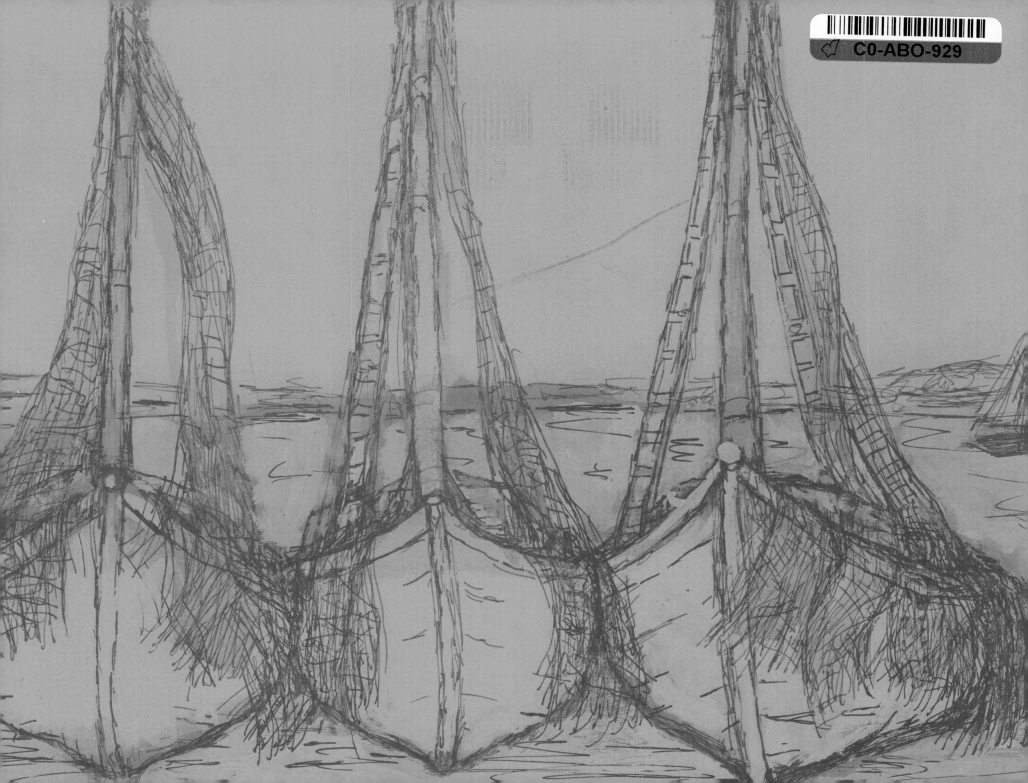

70869

Ile de Bréhat

THE FLOWERING ROCK

Ile de Bréhat

THE FLOWERING ROCK

Text and Illustrations by FRANK KLEINHOLZ

UNIVERSITY OF MIAMI PRESS

Coral Gables, Florida

For Lidia

Frank

Contents

Prelude

The sun has risen. On the quay they are putting the pieces of morning together. The sailors are readying the boats; a few fishermen have taken their places on the rocks. A black dog goes sniffing around. Some tourists begin to form a queue for the vedettes that will take them to Bréhat.

Lidia, you have done it. Let's not fool each other. It was you who took the seed of an idea of mine (was it really mine? did you plant it too?), nurtured it, fed it, kept it growing for twenty years until now, this early morning at Pointe de L'Arcouest, we look at the Ile de Bréhat and the flowering of a dream.

I hope that those who may read these words won't rush off to Bréhat to look for our dreams among the rocks and the walks and the hidden springs. We brought our Bréhat with us. And we took it back with us that last day—after the lobster and the cider and the love under the rainy rooftop. Let them bring their own dreams!

Bréhat. It was all a dream. And, my love, that episode about "Le Chat et La Reine," it was a fantasy. It never happened. Like everything else, it was all a dream.

[8]

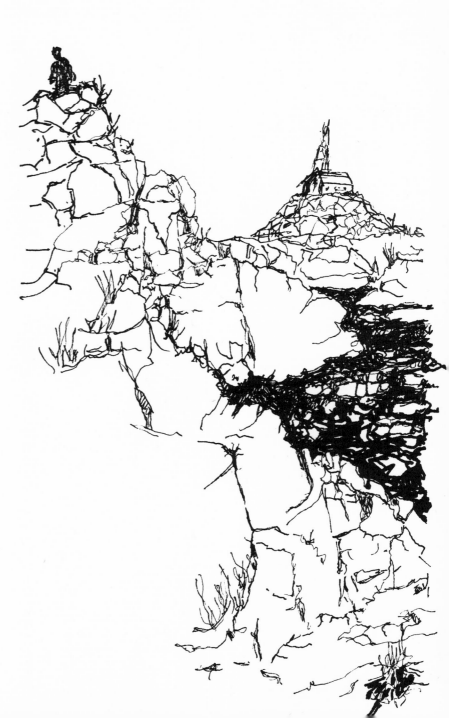

1 Strange How Things Happen

Paris . . .

Lidia and I were sitting on the terrace of the Rotonde having a Pernod and looking across at those who were sitting on the terrace of the Dôme having a Pernod and who were looking at us.

If I hadn't felt so lethargic, if the spring sun hadn't been so warming, I would have finished my drink, crossed the Boulevard Montparnasse and sat down by myself on the terrace of the Dôme. But I knew that if I went to all that trouble I'd be sitting there, looking at Lidia nursing her drink alone in front of the Rotonde. I would have taken all that trouble, faced the dangers of the traffic, just to find that it was as dull at the Dôme as it was at the Rotonde. So I sat where I was, slowly sipping my Pernod and watching the people pass by.

The scene changed dramatically as two pretty girls sat down at the next table and ordered two vermouth casses. They started to brighten up our corner with laughter. Their animated private talk was too fast for my hesitant French.

The words, "Ile de Bréhat" kept repeating themselves until I finally turned to Lidia, who with her high school French acted as family interpreter.

"What is this Ile de Bréhat they keep giggling about?"

She eavesdropped. Soon she was smiling too.

"It's a little island off the coast of Brittany, an island of flowers and rocks visited mostly by the French—les fleurs et les rochers is the way they put it. It's pretty and it's cheap. The dark-haired one says she had a love affair with a fisherman who kept plying her with lobsters."

"Do you like lobsters?"

"Who doesn't?"

"How about fishermen?" I asked.

"Collectively or individually?"

"That's your problem. Let's find out."

"What are we waiting for?" she asked.

"Let's go!"

We did.

It was as simple as that.

2 Ile de Bréhat

As places go the island was very small, no more than a mile wide and two miles long. Lidia put it this way: a dot on the map of Brittany. Within that dot a whole world existed. It was a world of religion, frustration, and despair tempered by the joys of everyday living: love, birth, marriage, feasts, holidays, and wine.

It was accessible from Pointe de l'Arcouest by vedettes, a fleet of small power boats that ran between Arcouest and Bréhat. There were no automobiles on the island; a few cows, a horse or two, goats, sheep, and a donkey. The only motors were the firetruck and the camion which hauled supplies to the hotel, the grocers, and the butchers and brought back the empty bottles to the port.

The island is divided into two, Ile du Nord and Ile du Sud, which are connected by a small neck of land called Pont ar Prad. The south island has most of the activity: Port Clos where the vedettes dock, Plage du Guerzido (the beach), le Bourg, the village square, the prefecture of police, the

[11]

mayor's office, the bowling green, and a few shops and bistros.

The Chapelle Saint-Michel sits on a bed of granite boulders some two hundred feet high in the northwest corner of the lower island and overlooks all of Bréhat and the surrounding sea. Off to the right of the Bourg is the old Norman church built in the twelfth century and added to through the centuries. A small cemetery nestles by its side.

One can walk from the southern tip of the island to the lighthouse at the extreme northern point leisurely in two hours. But the great charm of the island lies in its flowers and in its pink rocks. A lush growth of palms, mimosa, geraniums, fig trees, myrtle, oleander, roses, eucalyptus, and many, many other plants bedeck the island, thanks to its rich soil and the balmy Gulf Stream that bathes the island.

Archeologists can trace early origins of man here. Historians can relate the story of wars, warriors, and bloodshed from earliest recorded history down to the Nazi occupation.

Lidia and I leave that to the archeologists and the historians. We prefer to walk along the indented and broken coast, to look at the shapes and forms the pink rocks have assumed, to follow the labyrinth of paths, to get lost, and to know that if we walk long enough we will come to the sea.

We find our way to the old church and walk through the little cemetery, reading the headstones that tell of the

[12]

members of families who followed one after another to rest here. Small monuments and gravestones remind us that the Nazis had found their way to this island just a few years ago. This is a headstone in memory of a doctor who died in Buchenwald. This is the grave of a father and son shot by the Nazis. Not many as numbers go, but many when I think of the meager population of the island . . . The hand of fascism reached out and touched this little island and left its mark here, as elsewhere, in blood, tragedy, and death.

Porcelain flowers that carry the word "Regrets" are cemented to the grave beds, porcelain flowers that will never wilt, die, or be carried away by the wind. We leave a sprig of wild flowers on the graves of the martyred.

3 Thank you, M'sieur le Maire

Thank you for the old Breton house you found for us, the fireplace large enough to sleep in. The cistern, you say, is full, the roof tight, the outhouse clean.

Coal, wood, cider, still or sparkling, plumbing, odd jobs, hauling, besides handling the affairs of state: marriages, births, death certificates, and all the other forms and capers that the French bureaucracy has dreamed up. How does he do it all? When does he find the time?

We learned the hard way. He didn't. We learned to wait, and sooner or later, usually after we had forgotten what we wanted, he appeared and—"Voilà! "—here is what we wanted and needed weeks ago.

The rent?

"I told you it is one hundred dollars payable in francs for the month of August or for the year for that matter. Stay as long as you like. Nobody comes here before, or stays after August, so make yourselves at home. In August they all come: the tourists, the painters, and the writers. They dress like fishermen, row boats, and fish but they don't catch any fish. They don't fool us—no matter what they do they can't cover up their city ways. But who am I, an island mayor, to tell you, a painter, all this."

The house is an old Breton house. The lower floor has a kitchen with a wood stove, a dining room, and a sunny alcove leading to the courtyard. The fireplace is almost as big as the kitchen. We could toss a tree into it and later we did. There is a cistern to catch rain water, the only fresh water on the island; an outhouse, not too smelly; and a small garden with yellow roses climbing up the rock walls. Lidia and I choose the large upstairs bedroom for ourselves. The baby, Marco, will sleep in the alcove near us. Lolly will sleep in the other room. And Hélène, a young student whom we brought with us from Paris to stay with us and help with the children will sleep downstairs.

I place a table in front of the large window of our bedroom. It looks out upon a field of red poppies in a meadow of green. The Chapelle Saint-Michel sits on its mass of boulders overlooking the entire island and facing the sea. At this table I will draw and write.

The English Channel is about one-quarter mile behind us. The Isle of Jersey and the coast of England are not too far away. We are a short walk to the Bourg and to Port Clos.

Fields surround us, cattle graze, a few sheep and goats. Here and there farmers are working their fields.

Warns the mayor: "Don't drink the cistern water unless you boil it; don't drink the milk; the few cows here are tubercular. No one has ever touched the water except to bathe in it. Besides, sparkling cider is cheaper than bottled water and more plentiful. Why take a chance on the water? I deliver the cider right to your door."

Every morning I sit at my drawing table. I look out at the field of poppies. Again and again I draw the Chapelle Saint-Michel. Every evening a solitary cuckoo bird flies across the field singing, "Cuckoo! Cuckoo!"

I am obsessed with drawing. Lautrec said somewhere: "Forget drawing." But before you can forget, you must know. I had taken no oils with me, just paper, sketchbooks, pens, pencils, watercolors. I was going to draw and draw. I did. I never gave up on a drawing, not on the least little sketch. I worked it over and over. Good paper can take a lot of punishment. Whatever slickness that may have crept into the work was lost in the erasing and the redrawing. I had no need for models. Lidia was there, Hélène, the children, the fishermen, the fishmongers, and the trees, the bay, the harbor, the rocks and boulders, and, of course, the Chapelle Saint-Michel. The sketchbooks would fill up, the drawings

[19]

and watercolors pile up. It was the one way to measure time.

Everything was finally in place. Lidia had garnered some plates and kitchen utensils. We had brought our own linens. We were at home and that called for a celebration: a roaring fire, cider, a platter of sole fillets cooked by Hélène, a bottle or two of Muscadet wine. Afterwards Lidia and I, our stomachs full and a wee bit tipsy, went out to look for the lights of the English coast.

We found some boulders along the channel and sat down. We kissed some. Lidia looked out over the channel and said, "England is over there. See those twinkling lights."

"Yes," I said, looking into her eyes and kissing her again. The kisses grew longer as the night grew longer.

We were at home on this island. The light rain that began to fall was at first disregarded, but soon it could not be ignored.

"To be continued in our new bedroom," we pledged.

But when we got home the rain had found our bedroom before we had. Our bed was soaking wet. The ceiling was porous. We moved our bed here and there and finally located a dry spot. The children were moved into dry spots and their linen was changed.

How fragile is romance! How difficult to carry from under the stars into a wet bed under a leaky roof.

To hell with you, M'sieur le maire, and your house as tight as a drum!

[20]

4 City Fellow in the Country

I was born in a city, a big bustling city. I grew up in the city and moved from one city to another city. When I traveled it was to one city or another: New York, Chicago, San Francisco. Great cities, I felt. When I was lucky enough to travel abroad it was to London or Paris or Rome. Great cities, I felt. I love cities, so I felt.

And then suddenly I was removed from all cities. I was on an island—a little green and pink island in a sea churned up by volcanos and eroded by time, tides, winds.

There are no pavements, no cement, no big stores, no movies, no buses, no autos—just dirt paths, a lonesome cyclist, huge pink rocks over which lichen creeps. A handful of boats in the harbor turn over on their sides like Saturday night drunks and wait for the tide to return to straighten them out. A few cows graze in the fields, a tethered old goat munches away. Dogs run loose. I haven't seen a cat, which is strange. Perhaps cats are city fellows too.

In the city I would go from "here" to "there" as fast as I could. I never looked at or wondered what lay between "here" and "there." A face in the subway might take my mind off the "there" for a moment. But it was always "there" I was rushing to.

It took some getting used to this business of relying on your feet to get you from "here" to "there." And what was at the end of the road? After a while it didn't matter much. I learned to walk, to move through the fields and over the slippery rocks. I learned to see, to listen, to cherish surprises, to linger over new sights, colors, sounds.

The seagulls chatter and I look up at the ever-changing sky. A rabbit crosses my path and I look down at my feet and find wild flowers by the roadside. They are strangers. I have never met them before. I pick a few and study them.

Of course I knew the hydrangeas, the carnations, the climbing geraniums, and the roses, lusty blood-red and fragile pale-yellow. I knew the flowers that were cultivated in gardens.

But the wild flowers, those beautiful little nonentities that rested by the wayside or snuggled in the clover, they were strangers.

I picked little bouquets and I brought them home to Lidia. She knew about these things. She was a peasant. She knew the name of every flower.

She instructed me.

[22]

"What is this one? " I asked.

"Queen Anne's lace."

"And this one? And this one? "

"A gentian. A coquelicot—a poppy."

"And this dainty, beautiful one?"

"That, my dear, is a weed."

"A weed? "

"Don't be so sad," she consoled me, "weeds can be beautiful, too."

5 Strangers

We were strangers in Bréhat without benefit of a common language to form a tie with the people of the island, but we knew that if we were to have any joy in our stay we had to know them as individuals, as human beings.

Lidia, having lived in many places as a stranger, knew that she had to make the first gesture. She did her own shopping, knitting, and washing. She talked with the women in the marketplace and later visited and invited them in for some small talk and a glass of wine.

When the cistern failed to hold water, Lidia went to our neighbor and asked her advice. The woman told her that the cistern was not reliable. However, her son would help fetch water from the well. He did and we paid him. When he could not handle enough water for our needs his younger brother helped, and we paid him too. Soon there were volunteers telling Lidia where to shop, who was overcharging her, who was reliable. And after the island talk had worn out, Lidia talked about Paris, New York, the children, and often just the weather. When there was a birthday Lidia sent a gift. Soon they began to know her and she began to know them. The greatest sign of acceptance was when they told her that we were "serious" people. We worked—they suspected people who didn't work. No one came without a bouquet of flowers; no one left without some token of our high regard for them.

It takes time to build friendships, to remove hostilities, to achieve acceptance. We never rushed things; we waited for a gesture, a sign, and when it came we never ignored it—we accepted it and built on it.

The women of the island intrigued us most. They did the hard work while the men talked, drank, boasted, lived off their memories.

There were few old men, the old were women. They survived. The men took life easy and faded away.

Bréhat is a small world but it takes big women to carry it. There are no dishwashers, clotheswashers, refrigerators, servants, beauty shops. No movies, theatres. There is a butcher and a baker, and there are lots of fish to be caught, sold, and bought.

For movies and other pleasures they had to go to Paimpol by vedette and bus, some twenty-three kilometers away.

During August, the tourist season, a traveling circus with a few clowns, acrobats, a strong man, a side show, would take over the village square for a week. Then the whole town crowded the square, watched the acrobats, the clowns,

[26]

played the games, won a doll or a bottle of wine. There we laughed with our neighbors, shared our pommes frites, spun candy, and wine.

But it is the women who dominate the island in number, age, in commerce, in the fields, carrying the heaviest loads delicately balanced on their heads. They jog along, hands at their sides, greet, talk to others, laugh and joke.

They work the fields, tend the cows, shop for their daily food, nurse their babies, knit and mend, reknit and remend clothes, put patches on patches. The good black suit, the embroidered dress, the lace headress are carefully packed away, waiting for the grand occasion—a birth, a wedding, a funeral.

Strange phenomenon—the women work and slave and survive—the men talk and drink, take the easy life, decay, and turn to dust.

6 Fishermen

The fishermen—the fellows who left the dock before dawn in their grimy boats and came back after sundown and every so often failed to return at all—the fishermen seemed to be the key to the economy of the island. Most of the tourists come here for the mussels, the clams, the langoustines, the lobsters, the crabs, the oysters. It took no time to find out that fish were not cheap. The mussels and clams were not too expensive but the lobsters and the oysters were almost prohibitive in price.

The owners of the oyster beds were rich and they looked it. The restaurant owners collected francs avidly. But the fellows who caught the fish did not look prosperous. Their homes were small and their families were large.

No, the fishermen did not look prosperous. They looked romantic. The old ones sat around talking and drinking. The younger ones, in their knitted stocking hats, in their blue Breton pullovers, in their trousers and boots, had their eyes open not for fish but for the young girls. They seemed to

[30]

spend their time casting for the young ladies and, more often than not, hooking them.

On every lonely turn, in every shady corner, under this tree or that, there they were—making love—in that ardent, all-engrossing way, oblivious to the passersby. Alone or in a crowd, they wasted no time—amour came first.

In the beginning I was always sketching them, but after a while the theme grew monotonous. I labeled my first drawing "Lovers," the second I called "More Lovers," and then "Once Again, Lovers."

When I quit I titled my last sketch: "When the Hell Do They Fish?"

7   The Postman—Mr. Somebody

"M'sieur le peintre," he said one morning as he delivered the mail, "may I see your paintings?"

I told him that I had no paintings, just some drawings and watercolors and if he were in no hurry he was welcome to look at some and share an early bottle of cider.

I let him look through one portfolio. He nodded in approval.

"I am somewhat of an artist myself," he ventured. "But I do not paint. I raise dahlias. Have you seen my garden?"

I had seen his garden. His garden of neatly arranged rows of dahlias of all colors and shapes was one of the most striking on the island.

"Of course," I replied, "your garden is the most beautiful on the island."

I shook his hand. "You are an artist. All of us who love color and beauty are artists."

"Thank you. C'est vrai. Vous êtes très gentil."

We got to talking about art and artists, French painters—Picasso of course. We spoke of the churches and the Calvaries, of Breton and Norman art. He was a knowledgeable fellow. I opened another bottle of cider.

[33]

I asked him if he had ever been to the Louvre.

"The Louvre? No, I have never been to Paris. I hardly ever get to Paimpol which is only twenty-three kilometers from here. Once in a while when there is a pardon nearby I go; otherwise I stay here and tend my garden. You see my wife, rest her soul, passed away ten years ago. I am alone, and if you are a gardener, a real gardener, you love your flowers as you would your children and you do not leave them. Besides, what would I do in Paris?"

"Here, I am the only postman. Every morning people greet me 'Bonjour m'sieur le facteur' and I answer 'Bonjour. I hope I bring you good news.' And every evening I bring them the late mail and bid them a good night.

"I know them all, their good, their bad, their secrets—I share their joys and sorrows. Once in a while they invite me in for a drink and on holidays they have a little gift for me.

"And," he said with a devilish smile, "There are some ladies who wait for me to bring them their mail. I bring them some of my most beautiful dahlias. There is one. I can't tell you who she is—she's married, you see, her husband is a great fisherman, fishes all the time—to her I bring the rarest and loveliest of my flowers.

"No, M'sieur le peintre, I know everyone on this island and everyone knows me. They wait for me every morning and evening. Here on this little island I am Mister Somebody.

"Who would I be in Paris: Mister Nobody?"

[34]

8 Le Docteur

We were glad to learn there was a doctor on the island. After all, Lolly was two years old, Marco one month. It was best to see the doctor and have him look after the children. We had heard that he had been the head surgeon of a large Paris hospital and had come to Bréhat to retire.

Lidia went to his home and spoke to him. Later she reported that he was a lovely old man—somewhere between seventy and seventy-five. Yes, he would take care of the children. He would take care of anyone who needed his help. Yes, he charged a fee, by the kilometer like a taxi driver. If you lived within a short radius of his home his fee was the equivalent of fifty cents American; farther, seventy-five cents, and so on up depending on distance. When he came he would look us all over.

He came, and we offered him a sweet drink. He accepted it and sat down to talk for a while. He told us about himself, his wife, now dead, and his daughter. She would visit in August and he would like us to meet her.

He loved this island. Here he had privacy and solitude. Here he could read his medical journals in peace. Here he could fish and swim. He loved to swim. Every day, rain or shine, he had his swim.

He looked at me and said: "So, you are a painter. How nice. Painters usually are good people."

"And you, my dear girl," he said to Lidia, "you are a teacher? A teacher of little children. You seem to be a good mother, too. Monsieur, you are a fortunate man."

He turned to the children. "And you my little girl? Tell me about yourself. Your age and name? 'Lolly!' How charming, and what beautiful French you speak—a veritable Parisienne. Here, let me look you over. Where did you learn to speak French so beautifully? Hmmm, chest fine, stomach fine . . . Oh, I see, you spoke every day with your concierge in Paris, Madame Mallard. You eat well? That's good. Oh, she has a wonderful orange-colored cat named 'Soleil'; well, if I ever get back to Paris I'll visit Madame Mallard. How are your bowels? They are firm? Good. Yes, when I visit I will take a look at her cat too.

"And now for the little son. What do you call him? Marco. Why Marco? Oh, I see, after the great traveler, Marco Polo. Ah, he has been circumcised. A little Jewish boy. In the American hospital in Neuilly? Who was your doctor? Yes, I

know him. A good man, a very good man. Our Marco seems to be in excellent condition. . . . You are Jewish then. Only monsieur? You are a Catholic? How interesting. My God, how the Jews have suffered. Will they ever know peace? It was a crime, a crime.

"Now my Marco, let us turn you over . . . Hmmm. Good. The children seem to be in excellent shape. A warning—don't buy any milk on the island. The cows are tubercular. Buy Swiss dry milk in Paimpol. And the water is bad. I suggest you buy bottled water. The best is l'Eau D'Evian. Remember the name, l'Eau D'Evian. You should have no trouble. The meat is good and we have a baker who bakes the most delicious bread.

"And Madam, how do you feel? No troubles to report?

Stomach, liver, bowels? They move well, not loose? That's good. Bowels, that is what you Americans have most trouble with. The wine does it. You're not used to so much wine.

"Monsieur, let me take a look at you. A recurrent pain in your stomach? Let me see. No tenderness. Could be gas. Well, looking at the size of your belly, I would suggest the best remedy for your pain would be to eat less and swim and walk more, but if it recurs let me know.

"Mon Dieu! I've been here two hours. I must get along. My fee is fifty cents at today's exchange. How the franc has dropped! Where will it end? Thank you. I hate to take money from artists, but it's a matter of principle. Everyone should be paid for their work. Doctors especially—yes, and artists too."

9 The Staff of Life, or, can Man Live by Bread Alone?

It was upsetting to have a doctor, an old man at that, point at my belly and tell me to eat less. That called for some heavy thinking, a revaluation of an entire way of life. The whole spectrum of eating, its romance, history, aesthetics, philosophy, all reduced to a simple query: can man live by bread alone? And, more important, can man live without bread?

Breakfast presents no great problem—a piece of bread, coffee, and, if the morning was chilly, a Calvados or two—hardly anything to disturb us.

But déjeuner, the midday meal, not "lunch" (what a word!), but "déjeuner," an occasion to live for.

We start with an assortment of charcuteries, cold cuts, or a paté, or fruits de mer: oysters, clams, crevettes. And Muscadet, that cold, clear, dry white wine of Brittany to wash it down. Then the fish, a sole or mussels à la marinade; again Muscadet to wash it down.

Hélène could take sole, fillet it, twist the fillets into a cone, put them in a pan, submerge them in crevettes and good Normandy butter, and come up with a work of culinary art. More Muscadet. Rest a moment and dream.

And then the main dish. It could be a tournedos, a côte de veau or porc, or a gigot. But that was a Sunday dish. Hélène would prepare the gigot in a deep pan and bring it to the baker. He would bake it in his oven. There were strict instructions: when to put it in the oven, when to take it out. At the precise moment his daughter Antionette would bicycle it over to us. What timing! Its skin crisp, the inside pink, the gigot would rest hot and steaming in a bed of white beans. Wash it all down with a beautiful claret (Sundays only!).

After the gigot we sit back and reflect on life, its meaning, its worth. Important questions occur to me: Shall I take a nap? Shall I fight to stay awake and work? The claret helps to straighten out my thoughts.

Yes, some cheese: a piece of Port Salut, Brie or gruyère, some Pont l'Evêque, Camembert? A good red wine for the cheese. And the bread and the butter! Oh, that baker—that boulanger! The doctor was right: what bread, what crust, what cheese, what wine!

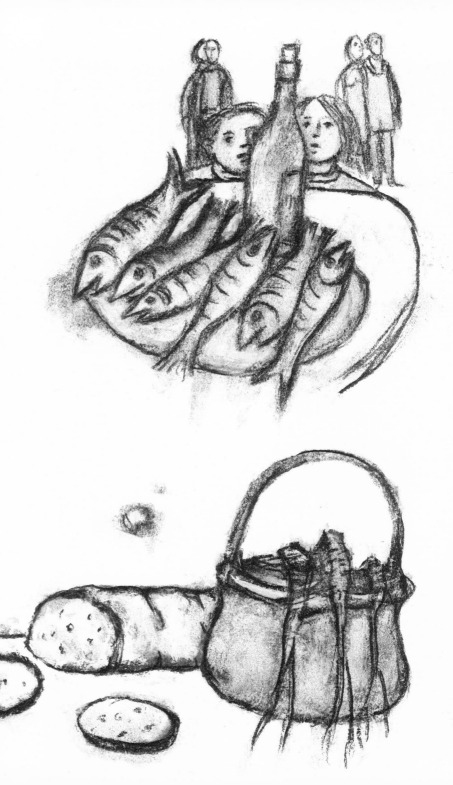

Fruit? Just a few grapes, a peach perhaps, that's all. Remember what the doctor said.

And café follows, dark and strong, a soupçon. A drop of cognac? Mirabelle? Cointreau? Don't take me so seriously. Fill the cup! That's better!

So, that was déjeuner. Now we can return to our philosophical inquest. Can man live by bread alone; can he live without it?

Yes, I think man can live by bread alone. If M'sieur Martin is the boulanger who bakes it. A baker who never seems to leave his oven. Always the flour-grayed shirt and pants, flour on his face and in his hair.

Lidia said that the easiest way to lose weight was to cut down on bread, or better still do without it. If I were the only one involved it would not raise any serious problems. But I was not. Suppose I had stopped eating M'sieur Martin's bread? And what if others took my example and also stopped eating M'sieur Martin's bread? What would become of him? Of his hardworking wife? Of his pretty daughter Antoinette? Would he go bankrupt? Would they be thrown out on the street? Would his wife leave him? And Antoinette. What would become of her? Would she take to the streets—a life of sin? No! No! I could go no further.

[41]

No, I could not have the fate of these three beautiful people on my conscience.

Have no fear M'sieur and Madame Martin, and you, pretty little Antoinette, you will not suffer on my account, belly or no belly. I cannot let you down.

Yes, man can live by bread alone, but he cannot live without it—that is, if M'sieur Martin is the boulanger.

10 "We Are Old, So Old"

I always went to Madame Marie to buy artichokes. She must have been the oldest person on the island, around eighty-five, I'd guess. It was hard to tell, for she was small, wiry, and full of sparkle. I never saw her face in repose. Her eyes were blue and dancing, and there was always a smile on her lips. Even when she was on her knees tending her field of artichokes she was smiling as if listening to some inner voice telling her amusing stories. She worked her patch with a big butcher knife, which she wielded like a grand sword. When she talked she unconsciously flayed it about, and it was wise not to get too close to her. I never saw her without that knife.

She would cut the artichokes, wrap them in newspaper, and then say, "Reposez-vous. Sit down a while; I want to talk.

"Do you mind? Nobody wants to listen to us old people.

Why? Don't we die fast enough for them? They can't wait to get rid of us. Haven't we earned the right to live out our lives?

"I heard that the Eskimos leave their old ones out on the ice floes to die in the cold. And you Americans, so kind and efficient, you send them to rest homes to be cared for by strangers. It's true, isn't it? True as I live and breathe and we are going to live and breathe to spite them. Do you know why? Because we work. We live by work and we love. We love the soil and the fruit of the soil. Take my artichokes—

have you seen more beautiful artichokes than mine? All meat and pink, no prickly fuzz. Have you had my artichokes with vinegrette sauce, the tops cut away and the rest sitting there like a great big rose in your plate? Have you eaten them cold with cloves of garlic hiding among the leaves? Anyway you eat them, is there anything better, more satisfying, tastier?

"You know I speak the truth, don't you? You are a wise man; you know the truth.

"Ah, you should have come here twenty, thirty years ago. Before the hotel and the tourists. Before our young became restless. It was something to see. We had some wonderful young then, workers and lovers. We wore our lace every Sunday and that little church was full of worshippers. Today it is broken, looted, empty. No one climbs up there anymore except a tourist now and then to take a photograph.

"Yes, we had wonderful young people then. Today the bold ones, the seekers, leave for the big cities. There is no future in the soil for them. Only the sluggards and the fools remain. And who comes here to stay? Some fancy old folks to retire? Some tourists, hotel people, waiters, cooks? When the season is over they drift away. What a life! To be the servants of tourists. And that is all that is left. Nobody comes here to make a life, to raise a family, to build a home, to work the soil.

"That's God's truth. I'm glad I'm old, and I'm glad I can work and grow beautiful artichokes for you. Oh, it's all true, isn't it? Come by again, M'sieur le peintre. I like you. You listen."

Every word she spoke was true.

11   Are You Happy With Us?

The mayor dropped by with a choice bit of news—the Quintals' baby was about due. The postman was disappointed that he was not the first to bring us the news about the Quintals but he came by and added a morsel. She was going to the hospital in Paimpol to have her baby. That was news on the island. Usually the midwife delivered the baby. Times were changing.

The women came by. Madame Quintal and her expected baby were the news of the hour.

"I hope it's a boy. The island needs more men."

"It will be the first addition to Bréhat this year." ·

Lidia went over to see Madame Quintal to wish her well. She brought her a small bottle of perfume.

"Good luck. What do you wish for? "

"A boy."

M'sieur Quintal was the cock of the walk. He strutted around the island talking and gesturing, accepting good luck drinks until his face was as red as the setting sun and his breath as potent as the inside of a wine barrel.

The day came when M'sieur and Madame Quintal stood on the quay at Port Clos waiting for the vedette to take them to Paimpol. Surrounded by luggage, the Quintals—she big with her nine-month load—boarded the little boat and off they went to our goodbyes.

"Bring back a boy!" someone shouted, "A boy!"

This time the postman beat the mayor with the news.

"Yes, it's a boy! Old man Quintal is the father of a boy. How did he ever do it?"

They were welcomed home in triumph. M'sieur Quintal had more free drinks than he could carry home.

He came over to invite us to the church for the christening. Of course, we went. We felt honored that we were invited.

After the church ceremony we were asked to their little home. Madame Quintal sat in the old upholstered chair receiving her guests. Wine and cakes were passed around. The

baby was ogled at, smiled at. Compliments were given to Madame and Monsieur, who beamed and laughed and could not keep their eyes off their little son.

There was something special in the air. We felt it and we knew it centered around us. We soon found out. There was a lull in the talk. M'sieur Quintal raised his glass and looked at Lidia and myself. The guests raised their glasses. All eyes were on us. We raised our glasses too, waiting.

M'sieur Quintal, bashful and hesitant, looked at us and said, "My dear friends, we are honored by your presence. We hope that you are happy with us."

He spoke with such disarming honesty and simplicity that for a moment I did not know how to answer him. I put my arm around Lidia and, facing them, said:

"Happy with you? My dear people, of course we are happy with you. For months we have wondered whether *you* were happy with *us!* "

I walked over to Quintal and we embraced in the good French way: a kiss on each cheek.

12 Pardons and Calvaries

Hélène told me that there would be a pardon at Sainte-Anne Aurey Sunday. If I wanted to go I had better get my boat ticket today. I had been waiting for a pardon to take place in some nearby town and Sainte-Anne Aurey was only a few miles down the coast.

Pardons are essentially Breton, a religious ceremony with a thousand years of tradition behind it. Here the faithful come to seek forgiveness for their sins, the sick for cure, the poor and bewildered for help.

Sunday we packed our lunch and Hélène and I, with a goodly number of the townspeople dressed in their finest black, women with their lace headdresses, aprons colorfully embroidered, men wearing their beribboned felt hats, all carrying their lunch, took our places in the vedettes that would take us to Sainte-Anne Aurey.

Sainte-Anne Aurey was a very small town built around an old and beautiful Romanesque church that dated from the twelfth century. It had a beautiful Calvary.

There are many Calvaries scattered about Brittany, small granite monuments depicting episodes of the Passion, the subject centered about Christ crucified on the Cross.

They say that the village stonemasons carved them. They are such marvels of piety, expressiveness, charm, and naiveté that one wonders where the artist began and the artisan left off.

Granite is the most durable of stone, the most difficult to carve. Modern sculptors shy away from it, but the Breton stonemasons took the granite boulders from the shore or wherever else they found them and carved them. What a struggle it must have been between the obstinate Breton stonemason and the granite that refused to conform to his chisel.

The stonemason won, and we, with all our modern tools, our pneumatic drills, can only stare and marvel at his ability and determination and wonder how he did it.

It is the procession that we all looked forward to. It began to form at the church at the top of the hill. Priests; monks; brothers in full vestments, red, white, purple, black; acolytes; choir boys in white; crosses; candles; effigies of Saints held aloft.

The prominent laity dressed in their finest led the procession. The women and young girls in their local costumes, lace headresses, embroidered vests and aprons,

[52]

multicolored petticoats, and their embroidered shoes followed. The elderly wore black dresses and colorful embroidered shawls. The young men wore embroidered vests, white shirts, flat beribboned felt hats. Flocks of children scrambled around between everybody's feet.

The street is so narrow that I have no room to stand. I either join the procession or run before it. I lost Hélène. I was so busy looking that I had no time to sketch, just a few hasty notes to be reworked later.

The places are taken. The crosses, the candles, the Saints shouldered, voices are raised in song. The procession starts and winds its way around the village square. Hucksters have set up stands around the square and are selling souvenirs, religious objects, candles, ices, drinks, and crêpes.

The church doors open to the light and to the procession. We enter. Voices fill the church and ricochet off the old walls. Candles, Hosts, and crosses bob and weave. The altar is fully illuminated. Everyone takes his seat and the Mass begins.

This is faith, the complete oneness of self and belief. You talk to your God, to His Mother, to your patron Saint. You talk to a myriad of spirits, fairies, demons all living here on the Brittany coast.

The Saints are counted by the hundreds, most of them never dreamed of or heard of in Rome. But here they live and breathe. Here they defy time. No one knows when they were born and no one doubts that they will live forever. There are patron Saints for the towns; there are healing Saints for every human ill from rheumatism to baldness.

I have always been a "smiler." I smiled a skeptical smile whenever I encountered an expression of deep faith. I looked down at anyone who in this twentieth century still believed in demons and goblins, spirits, and saints. Talk to God, talk to His Mother, beg for favors, what nonsense!

But there was a day long ago when a doctor told me that my wife, my young and beautiful wife, was going to die. She would die soon and there was nothing anybody could do about it.

I walked down Seventh Avenue toward my studio on Bleeker Street in New York in despair and bewilderment. The finality of his statement was too black to accept. I went from one bar to another (my civilized counterpart of a haven, a sanctuary, a church). At the corner of Fourteenth Street and Seventh Avenue a revival meeting, brass band and all, was going full strength. I stopped and listened. When the preacher asked "Who will come to Christ?" I almost fell to my knees. I wanted to drain myself of tears, of my anguish, but I held back. I resisted.

That was the only time I lost my reserve, my detachment, my cynicism. But I never held that moment of weakness against myself, after all, I was drunk and it didn't count. . . .

[54]

Now, in Sainte-Anne Aurey, I stop at a small stand that displays an assortment of steel articles: knives, kitchen utensils. The fellow who is selling them is about twenty-four, light of hair, thin, about five feet eight. His green eyes are pierced at the center by pinpoints of black. I hesitate before his wares. He looks me over, smiles, and asks "American?"

"Yes, how do you know I am an American?"

"You look like an American, that's all. Welcome. You are seeing the real Brittany today. I am a Breton. We are not French, you know, we are Celts. We were a great nation, with our own language, our own customs, ways. We have our own writers, our own literature, our own music. I, and others like me, am working to restore Brittany's independence. We will get rid of the French even if it means giving up our lives. We can make steel. These knives were made in Brittany. We feed France our meats, our fish, and our religion—our own Catholicism, not the decadence that France calls Catholicism.

"Our Holy Father knows that in all France there is only one people that are the true believers, one people that live by and for the Catholic Church, one people who are the soldiers of Christ, who will sacrifice all for Him. We are His children, we the people, young and old, of Brittany."

He grew more intense, more livid. His eyes bore through me. I get a queasy feeling of fear in the pit of my stomach. I can't get away from his drilling, fanatic, fantastic green eyes.

"Are you a Catholic? Do you believe in Christ, our

[55]

Saviour? " He knew I wasn't and I wasn't going to lie about it.

"No. Sorry," I mumbled. I beg off, break away from his hypnotic state, and walk away.

Somehow I know in the very depths of me what his green eyes were telling me—that he would gladly kill me to save my soul.

I found Hélène near the dock. She was smiling and talking to a handsome young fellow. I doubt if they were talking about God, our Saviour, our Father in Heaven.

13 Le Chat et la Reine

Did the cat look at the Queen?

Did the Queen look at the cat?

Or did they in that one instant of time look at each other, think the same thought, and smile—that mysterious smile that has been around through all eternity?

When I looked at her I knew we both knew what we were thinking about. But I said to myself: "Idiot! Leave well enough alone! Forget it—put it out of your mind! "

After all, she was a Queen. A real honest-to-goodness Queen. And she had a certificate to prove it. It read: "Queen of Bréhat 19__." I never got a good look at the year but I knew the document was official. You can't mistake an official French document.

She was a Queen all right—she walked like a Queen, she acted like a Queen, her ash brown hair was always piled high on her queenly head. She doled out her smiles with a touch of condescension like a Queen. You would never guess that her mother was the village fishmonger.

Her mother said, "The worst thing that can happen to a mother is to have a daughter who is a Queen."

Daughters are supposed to help their mothers carry on the family business. But not the Queen. She would never be a Molly Malone singing, "Cockles and mussels, alive, alive, O! "

No, a Queen should not carry the odor of fish about her.

The Queen loved to come over to our place. We were different. Americans. We had interesting visitors and I was a painter, an American painter.

Lidia had her baby-sit for us, take care of the shopping, take Lolly off for a day, gave her a chance to earn some francs.

She was nice to have around. You know how we Americans feel about royalty. And besides, she was darn good to look at!

Every once in a while she would look at me and I would look at her and we both smiled—that tricky little old smile. We knew something no one else did. But, every time that happened I said to myself, "Idiot! Are you crazy? " I never answered myself—I wasn't too sure.

It was a warm sunny afternoon and I was hiking along a path I liked. I had some sketching material with me and I'd sit down on a rock, make a sketch or two and walk on. I wandered along, engrossed in the landscape and my water-colors, never seeing another soul. I was truly alone, alone

with the flowers, the pink rocks, the vistas of the sea, the stretch of rocky beaches. If you can call that being alone, I was alone. That was the way I liked it. Time had no meaning, no essence.

It was growing dark, but I meandered along. I turned toward home. I had almost reached the most desolate spot on the island near the lighthouse. The sun was setting, a splash of gold and yellows mixed with opalescent grays, all reflected in patches of darkening waters.

I saw her out of the corner of my eye. She was in back of me and walking at a pace faster than mine. I walked on, ignoring her. It wasn't very long before I heard her behind me. Then I heard her breathing rather heavily a step or two in back of me. Her regal hand reached out, touched my shoulder and I stopped. I knew I was being knighted. I turned, we embraced and slipped to the side of the path.

Somewhere I read that night brought on silence. But I learned that there was no silence. The night was full of sound—night sounds and love sounds: the squabble of a flock of sea gulls settling down somewhere for the night, the wind at my ear bringing wisps of ash brown hair to my lips, the growling of the surf and the beating of the sea against the rocks, the scratch of an insect crawling along a leaf. Some laughter tumbles along all the way from Arcouest, drifts across the bay, and mingles with our heavy breathing. We are

[59]

one with the running of the tides—trembling, trembling, a gasp and a small cry; a giggle and a sigh—a happy full sigh. We raise ourselves to our feet. We brush the shreds of grass, the heather, from our clothes. It is dark now. We stand very close to make each other out. The Queen touches her fingertips to my lips, turns away, and is gone. The ceremony is over.

I pick up my scrambled sketches, my drawing paraphernalia, and start for home. Instinctively I look up. The sky is full of stars. I start to count them.

14 How to Make Bouillabaisse— The Easy Way

Hélène brought him home with her one day. His name was Roger, a mate on a fishing smack tied up at Paimpol. He sure was a handsome fellow: tall, dark eyes, and black, long hair, a yellow stocking cap, sun-paled dungarees, a striped Breton shirt, a blue sweater. Boots too.

He was a picture-book sailor if I ever saw one, down to the Gauloise Blue cigarette that perpetually dangled from the side of his mouth. If it weren't for his bad teeth he'd be a dream boy, but you can't have everything, can you? Hélène had brought back a good catch for herself.

"Could you put him up for a few days? "

"Where? " We were crowded as it was.

"Oh! He can sleep anyplace."

That was what bothered me most. Roger looked as if he could sleep anyplace—and with anyone.

But I could not refuse Hélène. She had been so good and so faithful to us. Besides, who could ask a lovely young girl to throw a catch as rare as that back into the sea. He stayed.

He was lots of fun, played with the children, did odd chores around the house, went off with Hélène on long walks. And every so often he brought home a bottle of wine. Most important, Hélène was happy and that made us happy.

"If you will permit, my friend," he said one morning, "I would like to take you fishing with me—a different sort of fishing. We carry only a basket for our catch and a knife. If we are lucky and get some good fish I will make the best bouillabaisse you have ever eaten, and that goes for Marseille where they are supposed to make the finest."

I had nothing to lose, so we got some baskets and a couple of knives. I put on a pair of boots and off we went!

The idea was simplicity itself. We went down to the bay as the tide was heading out. The tides rose and fell by as much as forty or more feet. They ran out with great speed and came back just as fast. At low water the sea bed was uncovered and reached out for miles—immense areas of shore were exposed. The trick was to walk behind the retreating tide, to follow the sea as she lifted her skirts with wanton abandon and rushed to the horizon. We walk as she retreats, our knives and baskets at the ready, looking for the laggards, those left behind: fishes in a pool of muddy water, crabs, lobsters dreaming. We pick them up and put them in our baskets. Simple, isn't it?

[62]

Roger led the way and I followed. He showed me the abalones welded to the rocks and I pried them loose. We netted six fair sized fish in one small pool. He reached under a rock for a small octopus, which proceeded to wrap itself around his wrist, its tentacles clamping viselike. I watched him as he took his knife, cut away the tentacles, picked up the squirming little monster, and threw it into his basket. He shrugged his shoulders and smiled: "This will make a tasty morsel for our bouillabaisse."

He knew where to look for eels. "You can't have a bouillabaisse without eels," he said.

It didn't take very long. In a few hours we had our basketful of fish, octopus, abalones, eels, some crabs, and, as luck was with us, three good lobsters.

"That is enough for a feast. And now back we go. We don't want to be caught by the incoming tide—it's not due but let's not take any chances."

We covered our catch with seaweed and headed for home where we would proudly display our haul.

They were waiting for us. Lidia, Hélène, the Queen, who had been dragooned to help, Lolly, and Marco. The catch was dumped into the kitchen basin: a squirming, fighting mess of fish, lobsters, octopus, crawling eels.

"My God! " from Lidia. "What in all hell are we going to do with this ungodly mess? "

[63]

"Make a great bouillabaisse, my dear lady. I will make it, you girls will help, and before you know it, we shall be feasting," said Roger.

"Now, to begin, make a big fire in the stove. You, Hélène, get some wood and get the fire going. You, Queen, get the largest and heaviest pot and fill it with three liters of water and get it boiling. You, Madame, chop three cloves of garlic fine and fry them golden brown. Take one onion, peel it—you have an onion, good! Pierce it with three whole cloves, place it in the boiling water with a few leeks, toss in a bouquet of fresh thyme, some salt and pepper. That's all for now—we must keep it simple, we don't want to get this complicated. Let it simmer for a half hour, and I will put some bottles of Muscadet in the cistern to chill.

"Remember, we don't want to overcook anything! Everything must be slightly undercooked!

"Now, Monsieur, we must clean the fish while the water comes to the boil. Here take my fish knife, clean out the insides of the fish, scrape off the scales but don't touch the heads. The fish must be whole, bones, head, tail, all except scales and innards. And then start peeling the eels."

"Who, me? "

"Yes, you! "

Have you ever peeled an eel? Do people actually peel eels? Was Roger putting me on?

"Why peel the eels?" I asked him.

"Because the skin is too fat—so we must peel the eels."

"Me?"

"Yes, you!"

All through my life, through vicissitudes, happiness, tragedies, I had never dreamed that I would one day peel an eel. An eel? There were six of them, live and squirmy. I never liked eels anyway, and here I was peeling them.

I looked at Roger. No, he was serious. I started to peel my first eel.

When he came back from the cistern he looked at me and took a hand. Things went faster then.

The water was boiling, the garlic simmering. "The fish and eels go in first, they take longer to cook" said our Master Chef, Roger.

"God! Will I ever be able to get this fish smell out of the house? I feel it in my hair, on my skin, my hands. How crazy can you get?" This from Lidia, who never was a fish fancier and from today on would be less so.

The Queen didn't say a word.

"Don't worry, chère Lidia, the smells will change—from

fish smells to the smell of the sea and then to ambrosia. Have faith in me" begged Roger.

"It had better change."

"Hélène," again said Roger, "take out the leeks and the herbs and put in the fish and the eels and watch them—remember no overcooking! "

Hélène looked at him. Now she knew she had found her true love. He had not asked her to clean the fish or peel the eels. He had maneuvered it so that I would be the one cleaning the fish and peeling eels. Take me down a peg or two—any time I wanted to impress them with my importance all they had to do was remember me struggling to hold and skin a live, squirming eel.

It was true; with the smell of garlic, thyme, onion, leeks all mingled with the sea-fresh fish the kitchen began to have a heavenly aroma and our stomachs responded, our mouths began to water, and there were still the shellfish to add to the pot.

"Out with the fish and into a warm pot, cover it, and keep it on the far side of the oven."

"Now, the lobsters and the crabs, till they are pink—pink, not red. And now I will make the sauce."

Again the Master Chef, a Gauloise Blue hanging from his lips, takes a copper bowl and in go four egg yolks, a half

bottle of Muscadet, a zest of lemon. He beats it up and lets it simmer.

The steaming fish is now in our large old soup bowl. He strains the broth, adds the thick sauce, and pours it over the fish, with a pinch of saffron for color. Crabs and lobsters are placed on top of the dish—a crown of glory!

The dishes are in place, warm and ready. The bouillabaisse crowned with lobsters and crabs rests in the center of the table. The Muscadet is well chilled, the glasses large and clean.

Roger takes a spoonful of the broth and passes it to me: "Your honor."

I taste it. It is good; it is damn good. It is nectar, it is great. I wash it down with a drink of Muscadet and, addressing the Master Chef, I take two claws and the tail from a lobster.

"Master Chef, I award you two ears and the tail! "

Later, much later, we are having some Calvados to round out the evening and we tell the girls of our exploits: how we caught the fish in the retreating tide. Roger laughingly tells about his life-and-death struggle with the octopus and then becomes very serious.

"My dear children," he says, "listen very carefully. It took only three and a half hours from the moment we deposited the fish in the basin until we were ready to sit down at the table. In Marseille, they take seven hours. I have eliminated at least four herbs, some special fishes, all nonsense anyway, and we had no difficulty in preparing a most delicious bouillabaisse. It was good, wasn't it? And above all, très simple."

15   Lidia! We are Rich!

It was my turn and I didn't like it. Monday, and my turn to clean up the house. Beds to be made, floors to be swept, dishes to be washed, and—worse—chamber pots to be emptied and washed.

But there was nothing I could do about it, no way I could avoid it. A bargain is a bargain, and I had agreed to clean up once a week, and Monday was my day.

All those bottles after the weekend: wine bottles, cider bottles, empties of apertifs, and beer bottles; all had to be collected, rinsed, and put into their cases. There was a deposit on each bottle and they were valuable.

I was a wonder with the broom. The broom was a thatch of twigs held together with a band of wire, no doubt made this way for centuries but an efficient instrument, nonetheless. But bed making was my problem—I just couldn't make up a bed properly. Lidia and Hélène didn't let me forget it either. They always redo the beds after me, even if it only is to straighten out a corner of the bed cover, never failing to remind me that as a housekeeper I am a total loss.

I do the beds first—fast—the way I like to work: get the toughest part of the job out of the way first; the rest will then seem easy.

The bottles were a pleasure, usually some dregs were at the bottom of the bottles. These I poured into a large jug. It makes a potent drink and helps when I get around to sweeping the floors, at which I am a fiery demon.

It also fortifies me for the next chore—emptying the chamber pots. I never realized we had so many. Gingerly and daintily I carry them downstairs and line them up in the sunshine outside the kitchen door. I can only take one out at a time, that's how full they are—mute testimony to a wonderful weekend of drinking. I am careful, not spilling a drop. If I spilled any my superiors, Hélène and Lidia, would have something more to add to their complaints about the quality of my work.

Carefully, carefully, this Monday morning I line them up one by one in the courtyard outside our kitchen window before dumping them into the outhouse. I stand there for a moment resting and counting. Believe it or not, there are ten

chamber pots, all full, sitting there trembling golden in the sunlight.

I stand there thinking and dreaming. And in that moment a great truth dawns upon me—now I know myself as I had never known myself before—I "find" myself as they say. I know that I am one with all the collectors; the collectors of objets d'art, collectors of stamps, collectors of books, collectors of dollars, collectors of buttons, comic books, matchboxes, collectors of old newspapers, magazines, collectors of pieces of string. Compared to me they are all nothing. Their collections seem meaningless, for at that moment I realize that I am the owner of the largest collection of piss in the world—unique—the only collection of its kind. I can visualize the auctioneers at Sotheby's or Parke-Bernet and the frantic bidding of the world's greatest collectors for my precious collection.

I can hardly pull myself away—all these chamber pots brimming yellow in the sunlight—all that goddam golden piss. And it is mine, all mine.

I must share my good fortune with somebody—it is just too much for me to hoard for myself: I turn and run looking for Lidia. I find her and drag her through the kitchen door to the courtyard, to the chamber pots full of liquid gold.

"Lidia look, look Lidia," I cry, "Look! We are rich! "

[71]

[72]

16 Tourists—
Nobody Wants to be a Tourist

Nobody ever wants to be called a tourist.

I felt happiest and most secure when my neighbors accepted me as one of their own. No doubt, when we left, they talked about us as the foreigners, the Americans, the tourists.

The tourists swarm off the vedettes. After fifteen minutes on Bréhat they are at the café tables looking at the new arrivals disembarking and saying one to the other, "Look at the tourists!"

I sit, just removed from the tourists, and smile at them too. After all, I'm an old-timer, an old settler—I've been here all of three months.

There are few American tourists here. They seem to cling to the big cities and get no further in Brittany than Mont Saint-Michel. The few foreigners are mostly English, but there are some Dutch and a scattered few who have lost their way and stumbled onto this place.

But the French know about it. They love the fruit de mer, the seafood, and here they get it fresh from the sea.

They can buy crêpes made over a small brazier and filled with ham, shrimp, or sugar. They can swim, sunbathe on top of rocks, become part of nature's sculptures. They can walk in fields of flowers, see gardens bursting with climbing geraniums, roses, dahlias, daisies. They walk secluded paths, linger in hidden, sheltered nooks. The couples lose themselves, and if you are not careful, you step on them.

Beginning with Bastille Day and through the month of August the tourists swarm like bees over the island. The children, the tots, are herded by the grandparents while mama and papa look for their lost love among the hidden patches of green. There are dogs, little dogs and big dogs, every breed, over-loved and spoiled.

The teenagers flirt and laugh and love. No traffic to worry about—only two vehicles, the fire truck and the camion that

moves the potables, loaded with cases of wine, beer, cider, apertifs of every color, and back with the clanking empties. The busiest man on the island: back and forth all day and far into the night to meet the boat, pick up the full cases, return the empties, pick up the full cases—a never-ending cycle of incredible thirst.

I could never understand the prejudice against the tourists. They are today's pilgrims. The shrines have changed, they look at the old churches, the Calvaries, Mont Saint-Michel, the monuments of the past to be looked at and wondered at. But the faith that created them is gone and cannot be retrieved. Today the shrines are the beaches, the sea, the sun, laughter, food, and love—always love, always careless love.

The girls chase the boys. The boys chase the girls. The manly women with the sad-faced, well-dressed girls. The middle aged with their young man or young girl in tow. The families: middle class, poor, picnicking in the fields, on the beaches. Why not? In one way or another it's all l'amour! Who am I to object? Who writes the script? They do—they are writing it for now, for today.

All year long the islanders wait for these six weeks. The souvenir shops, the bistros, the hotels, the restaurants, the grocers, the tobacco shops. After these six weeks, most of them close up and go back to where they came from, for they too are tourists. They live off the tourists and they gripe about them. Says one: "Everything is too expensive for them. I tell them: 'If you have money nothing is expensive, if you have no money everything is too expensive. Go somewhere else if you have no money.'"

Yes, it's take it or leave it, that is during the six weeks of vacance. But come September, when the shutters are up on almost every shop and the shopkeepers sit around counting their francs, they talk to each other: "Did you have a good summer?" Which means: How much money did you make? And they will sit around living off their summer francs and wait for the next summer. They are tourists too—the other side of the coin. Yes, most certainly they are tourists, and no disgrace. After all, in one way or another we are all tourists.

[76]

17 Le Mont Saint-Michel

Suddenly between a break in the trees you see it for the first time, and you cannot believe what your eyes tell you is there. A misty, hazy apparition rising out of the sea. Mont Saint-Michel. As you get closer it takes on form and reality—one majestic mass of Norman and Gothic architectural splendor, growing out of the massive boulders of granite that rest on the vast gray marshes. The figure of Saint-Michel, the Archangel, stands on the summit of the tower sky-high above us.

Lidia and I could never get enough of Mont Saint-Michel. We visited it often, but our visits were usually confined to the tourist season when bus tours were available. Finally we decided that we would spend a night or two on the Mont at Christmastime when it would be almost deserted.

And so it was. We arrived one December afternoon. There was not another car in sight, no tourists, no guided groups. A flock of sheep grazing in the marshes was the only life in sight.

It was cold; clammy, bitter sea cold. I had an old army
coat, stocking hat, heavy underwear, and boots. Lidia had
two sweaters, a heavy coat, a woolen kerchief around her
head, and her woolen-stockinged feet were encased in heavy
boots. We had prepared for the cold. Most of the hotels were
closed, but we found one that was open and we had an
omelet there. What omelets at Mont Saint-Michel—eggs
beaten in Normandy butter and fried in a copper pan over a
fire of slow-burning twigs.

Chauffage? No, they had no heat in the hotel, but if we
wished they would let us have an electric heater for the night
at a surcharge of one dollar. "Fine," we said, "put it in our
room; we are going up to the cathedral."

We were alone in the cathedral. Just the two of us, our
footsteps echoing through the empty halls. The concierge,
hearing us, thumped toward us in his wooden sabots,
wondering what we wanted.

Just to look around, alone, to stand on the parapet at
night. That is all, we told him. We tipped him and he
graciously left us alone.

We walked through the abbey, through hall after hall,
spotting the early Romanesque nave and the elegant Gothic.
Up the Lace Staircase and out to the gallery that overlooks
the sea from a height of over 250 feet. Just the two of us,

batted like a tennis ball back and forth from the year 800 to tonight and back again.

And finally the ramparts. The moon was out, the bay silvery gray twinkling with moonbeams. The wind was blowing from the north, from the sea, and it was biting, but that did not matter. What mattered was that we had done something we had dreamed of doing. We embraced and became a part of the unity that gave Le Mont Saint-Michel its grandeur.

What do you do, two alone, in love, the wind whipping your faces, the cold eating through your heavy clothes—two little people on this pile of rock that had been sitting here for over 1100 years. Here we are—two little people wondering how long into the future time would carry this monument, built by man not only for the glory of his God but for the glory of man.

We get back to the hotel to our icy room and under the bed covers as fast as we can. We turn on the tiny electric heater but no heat comes forth, but by then we really don't care. For, miracle of miracles, as we cling to each other we are enveloped by a wave of warmth, of heat—more than enough for two very little people.

18 Portents

The moment I saw the rock sitting there among the boulders that fronted the channel, I knew it was mine, my hideaway. It had been carved by the sea, shaped into a big bathtub; water filled it about three-quarters full. It was an ideal place to take a bath or just to sit in and meditate. It was hidden from the shore and it was there I would go on a sunny day, strip naked, and sit in my bathtub, light up a Voltigeur, and look out toward the Isle of Jersey and the English coast.

It was not too far from our house, a short walk across a field where four sickly cows and one goat grazed. I always said "good morning" to the goat or "good night" as the time of day required. We had so much in common—goatees and all. He would stop for a moment in answer to my greeting, look me in the eye, nod his old head, and return to his grazing. We exchanged greetings numberless times, and after several months he would be waiting for me to pass by and greet him; "Bonjour, M'sieur le chèvre."

My bath was an ideal spot to tie pieces of string together. I would sit there, smoking away, secure in my solitude, hidden from all eyes, picking out the strings I carry in the basket of my memories and tying them together.

Some strings were "yesterdays," some, "todays." "This morning," "this minute," and some, more fragile, were the "tomorrows." These I doubled up else they would come apart.

The strings had names too. This one was "Lidia"—a tough piece of string—this was "Lolly," this one "Marco," and this one kind "Hélène." And of course the "Queen;" she had coiled around my neck like the hair of the Medusa. A thin piece of string for Roger and his bouillabaisse, for Mr. Somebody the Postman, and some were strings that were tied to the yesterdays—Leah, my mother, my father, Joe, Humboldt Street, all the actors, big and small, dead or alive, who had become one with the skein of my life. What a ball of twine that would make—that is if all the strings could ever be tied together.

And these last strings, for the pink rocks, the trees, the sea, the flaming flowers—these I will weave into a garland for my Lidia's hair.

I will tie them all together—someday—but today they are bunched and raveled into one big knot.

When will I unravel them, when will the memories come

back to me? Next year? Two, five, ten, twenty years from now?

When a strange color comes to my brush will I recognize it as a color I first saw on Bréhat? Will I know where it came from? I think I will, no matter how old I may be at the time. You don't forget Bréhat so easily.

Why was I saving these old pieces of string? Could I help but save them?

Why was I saving all those scraps of paper, notes, drawings, sketches, watercolors—hoarding them?

Don't ask so many questions, Lidia tells me. Your work has a validity, an honesty. Paint, draw, work. . . .

But was that enough? Was that enough to hold things together, to justify a lifetime of struggle?

In a world of experimenters where every artist tries to make his own piddling revolution I keep on repeating old ancient simple truths. Like a good old rabbi I repeat and repeat what I think are eternal truths.

I ignore my friends who ask; "Aren't you ever going to change?" What change? Surfaces change. The tides change. The seasons change, but the sea remains. The flowers and the trees come and go and come back again. Today's faces are yesterday's faces—the cosmetics change, the deodorants change, but the sweat and the stink remain. The hairdo changes, styles change, but the same harried faces remain.

[83]

Like the pink rocks of Bréhat, they disappear here, reappear there.

I could never keep my big mouth shut, announcing to the world that this was it: I had found Nirvana! How many times have I found Nirvana and in how many places! For Lidia and myself they were Nirvanas even if they lasted a week, a month, or a year, but as soon as I opened my big mouth and told my friends and through them their friends that I had found Nirvana, they all flocked to share it with us. And in the process helped destroy it. Nirvanas cannot be shared.

I was happy when they came—it broke our lonesomeness—and happier when they left.

It had nothing to do with them. They brought echoes of Paris, New York; gossip, new stories, the latest jokes. But their presence polluted everything: work, concentration, isolation, love. They came, their numbers increased, their stays lengthened. The waters were being polluted.

And the autumn wind, the evening and night wind that now increased its intensity, was cold, piercing cold. It blew harder and colder and would increase as winter approached. Now it wailed and cried like a child at night; tomorrow it would moan like an old banshee. It penetrated clothes, bent and reshaped the pine trees, came through the smallest crack

[84]

in the wall or opening in the window, finally lodging itself in the very marrow of our bones. The wind was the sire of all the haunting legends of Bréhat. The wind was another portent.

And then there was that string of paintings, some resting in Paris, some in my studio in New York, some finished, some unfinished. They were calling to me: Papa! come home to us!

Those I thought completed bothered me most. Were they complete? Could I really say that I had finished this one or that one? I thought about them and I wanted to take another look. Now that time had separated us, now was the time to take a fresh look. Were they so complete that there was no place for another touch? I knew I had to go, look, and find out. And if I found one or two that said all that I had to say, to which I would never add or take away a speck of paint, I could look at them with that sense of fulfillment, satisfaction, completeness that only an artist knows.

In the deepest sense I doubt if a painting is ever "finished." A painter's career is a series of unfinished paintings. Invariably he starts out to say one thing and winds up saying another. Ah, but in the next one he will catch what escaped him in the preceding one, and if not this one, he will get it in the next one, or maybe the miracle will happen in

the one after that, the next one and all the next ones, until that very last one when the final brush stroke puts an end to all the next ones.

Tying strings together, pasting them together with spit, with questions. Always the questions and the search for answers. Must there be an answer to every question? Aren't questions fun enough? Are unanswered questions more fun?

It was time to see if Lidia had any answers.

I walked across the field. There was my friend the old goat, munching away. I walked up to him and said, "Goodnight, my dear friend."

I waited for him to return my greeting. He looked at me for a long time, a long time for a goat that is, nodded his head, and returned to his nibbling.

He knew and I knew that this was the last time we would say goodnight to each other.

[88]

19 Islands

I am an island. Lidia is an island. Lolly is an island. So is Marco and so are you.

Yes, we are all islands fighting the tides, the winds, the erosion, fighting to keep our heads above water. Our hands locked in the hands of other islands.

Lidia, I feel guilty. In my selfishness, I saddled you with all these chores. Lolly in this strange place is speaking such fluent French that we cannot understand her and so little English that she cannot understand us. She is drifting away from us. And Marco, a little baby. We were lucky, no illness. Will our luck hold out? Should we chance staying on? For myself, I've walked the island from end to end. I've made hundreds of drawings, watercolors. I want to share my work with others now, to show my work, and above all I'm dying to take a look at my paintings finished and unfinished.

And money, dear girl, that rare commodity. No, there are no free rides on this merry-go-round, artists not excepted. My dealer in New York had sent me remittances from sales he had made, and when sales dropped off, he sent remittances against future sales and then just loans, plain ordinary loans. I had no paintings to send him and would not have any until I got back to New York. He was a good fellow who understood and wanted to help me, but his letters showed that he was hurting, and I knew that soon the hurt would overwhelm the kindness. After all, he wasn't in business for love—only lovers are in business for love.

We were too long away from the mainland, too long away from the bustling life, the give and take of fellow artists, of shop talk and galleries and museums, and from exhibitions and a few sales.

Lidia, it's going to be sad parting with all the roses, the dahlias, the fragrant eucalyptus, the palms, the daisies, the wild flowers, that solitary cuckoo bird and the old goat, the postman and Madame Marie, the blackish-green blue sea full of fishes and lobsters and crayfish and crabs and mussels; the bathing at dawn, the swims by moonlight; the ever-changing skies, the moon full with child; the rushing tides, those heavy tides that creep up to the high-water mark and stop there just when we think it will overwhelm us and sweep over the island.

It will be a sad parting, but I know we will be back. I say to Lidia, "I know it—I feel it—someday we will come back here!"

"We'll talk about that when the time comes," said Lidia, "Now let's start packing!"

20 The Flowering Rock

Pack, pick up and go. To leave, tear ourselves away from newly found beauty and love.

Put it all in boxes, packages, bundles. Have the camion waiting, take it all to the port and pile it on the vedette and then into a car. Carry it all to Paris and there, take the pieces apart and put them together again, and then take them apart and to New York and who knows what other place and places.

How much can we carry with us? What do we take, what do we leave behind? What will remain of it after the journey? Will the flowers, the friendships, the memories survive the journey? How will they take to the smell, the dust, dirt, and rot of the cities? Is there some preservative, some magic elixir that will enable us to take and carry the few minutes of ecstasy Bréhat gave us?

Rocks, stones. They are here piled in a corner. Lidia has collected and saved them. Here they have been resting and waiting, a mute tribute to Lidia's love for Bréhat and her desperate attempt to cherish it, save it, take it with her, corporally, physically. They are more than symbols, more than souvenirs. They are the soul and guts of Bréhat. Things to see, touch, smell—something concrete, existent, a piece of Bréhat to carry with her.

Small rocks, medium-sized rocks, large rocks. Rocks polished mirror-smooth by the sea through countless ages. Rocks covered with barnacles, lichen. Rocks bearing the white handwriting of prehistoric worms, rocks bejeweled with fossilized snails. Rocks with a seed of green carrying tomorrow's flower, and, of course, a flowering rock.

Lidia, my lovely Lidia, what are we to do with all these rocks?

Take them with us? We have two children, and my work, Hèléne, and God knows what else—all in one tiny automobile. And suppose we can transport these rocks to our little place in Paris—what then? How will we get them home, to the studio on Bleeker Street?

Must we take them all, every single rock and stone? Can't we take a few? I will paint some flowers on this rock, a face or two on this one. Shall we take these two and leave the rest?

Remember, we found flowers before we ever heard of Bréhat—and in the most unlikely places, the most hostile of soils. In the streets of Brooklyn, Greenwich Village, in the

[92]

cobblestones of Paris, flowers in the strangest places growing, denying death, affirming life.

We will find flowers wherever we go. No need to hang these around the neck of our memories.

Lidia looks at me—silent, silent for a long time, and then she says thoughtfully, quietly: "Les fleurs et les rochers—the flowers and the rocks. Remember, those were the words the girls used on the terrace of the Rotonde when they spoke about Bréhat.

"And do you remember that day, after we had come here, unpacked? We took Marco and Lolly and climbed the hill behind the house. Our first sight of the sea. The Channel far below us and the sea pounding away at the rocky beach. Marco, on all fours, crawling on the carpet of moss, thick and soft. Lolly among the slippery rocks and I after her. Suddenly under my feet a flower growing out of a rock. I called to you—Frank! look! There are flowers growing in the rocks! Flowering rocks!"

"Yes, you are right. The flowers and the rocks. They are Bréhat, they belong here, let them remain. They are all of a piece. The flowering rock, it *is* Bréhat."

[94]

Epilogue

I spent the years 1948 to 1950 in France, working in Paris. On the first of May, 1950, one month after the birth of our son, Mark, my wife Lidia, my two-year-old daughter, Lisa, the baby, and I set out for the Ile de Bréhat on the Brittany coast. There we became part of the family of people on the island. The children thrived on the good sea air. I worked and filled sketchbook after sketchbook with drawings. After six months, and with much reluctance, we returned to Paris and shortly thereafter to the United States.

Some twenty years later the publisher saw my Ile de Bréhat sketchbooks and said he would publish them if I would write a story about our stay on the island. So in the summer of 1970, Lidia and I returned to Brittany. We nostalgically followed the same route to Bréhat, revisiting Chartres, Mont Saint-Michel, Saint Malo, Saint Brieuc, Paimpol, and l'Arcouest.

We spent two weeks at the Hotel Barbu at Ponte de l'Arcouest looking across the bay at Bréhat. My hotel window and writing desk faced the island. Every day for two weeks I sat at this desk writing. Then we crossed over to the island for the first time in twenty years and took a room at the Hotel Belleveu, where the window and writing desk faced l'Arcouest. The mornings were given to writing, afternoons and evenings to walks around the island.

Twenty years had not brought many changes to the island—some new summer homes, improvements in plumbing and in the fresh water supply. But the sea air had the same freshness, the same invigorating quality. The sea moved as relentlessly as ever and the tides charged today as yesterday. The water was the same green and purple and it piled up on the pink rocks as tirelessly as it had in the past. The fields were filled with brilliant wild flowers in reckless profusion, and the gardens were full of orderly rows of flowers of every hue and variety.

For us, nothing seemed to have changed.

With a few editorial corrections this is the book written at the Hotel Barbu and the Hotel Belleveu in the summer of 1970.